Windows 10 Maste
The Ultimate Window.
Mastery Guide

Jonathan Bates

CONTENTS

Introduction

I want to thank you and congratulate you for downloading *Windows 10 Mastery: The Ultimate Windows 10 Mastery Guide.* This book contains proven steps and strategies designed to ensure you have all of the information you need to ensure your Windows 10 upgrade experience proceeds as smoothly as possible while at the same making sure you know what to expect when the upgrade is complete with the goal of helping you to jump in to Windows 10 without any hesitation.

The following chapters will discuss what's required to get your upgrade or fresh installation of Windows 10 up and running. From there it's a discussion of Windows 10's new features including the enhanced search functions found in Cortana. After that there is a detailed explanation of the many ways you can personalize Windows 10 to increase productive, a note on new security features and a list of Windows 10 specific shortcuts. Finally, there is a list of advanced tricks for personalizing Windows 10 even more and getting the most of a Windows 10 device and Xbox One pairing.

Thanks again for downloading this book, I hope you enjoy it!

1 Get Started-Install Requirements-Upgrading to Windows 10

Windows 10 is unique among Windows operating systems in that it was designed with a wide variety of platforms in mind. Windows 10 runs on tablets, phones, personal computer and the Xbox One. Many common functions have been offloaded to the cloud on the less powerful platforms which means that users' content will be available in all places at all times.

Hardware Requirements
PC Windows 10 requirements include the following minimum system components:
- Windows 7/8
- 1GHz or faster processor
- 64-bit systems require 2 gigabytes of ram
- 32-bit systems require 1 gigabyte of ram
- 64-bit systems require 20 gigabytes of free hard drive space
- 32-bit systems require 16 gigabytes of free hard drive space
- A video card that works with DirectX9 or above
- A screen with at least an 800x600 pixel display
- 3-gigabytes of data downloaded from the internet

Requirements for mobile Windows 10 devices include the following minimum system components:
- 512 megabytes of available memory
- 4 free gigabytes of storage space
- Directx9 or above
- A functional back button, volume control, power button and start button
- 4 gigs of memory for phones with a 2560x2048 resolution
- 3 gigs of memory for phones with a 2560x1600 or 2048x1152 resolution
- 2 gigs of memory for phones with 1920x1080, 1920x1200 or 1440x900 resolution

- 1 gigs of memory for phones with any screen down to 800x480

Prepare to Upgrade

Windows 10 is free to everyone who is currently using a legally acquired copy of Windows 7 and Windows 8 and was designed to run well on laptops and personal computers designed to run using either system. Computers that are eligible for the upgrade will have a Get Windows 10 button in the lower right corner of their task bar.

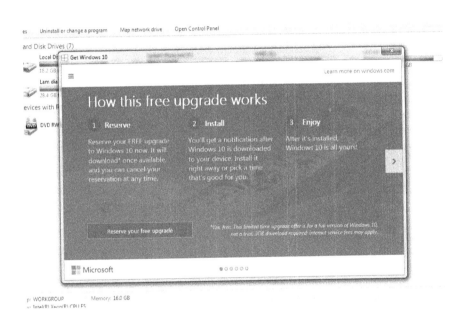

Check compatibility

Upgrading from one operating system to another is a fairly straightforward process, which means many of your applications files and settings will transfer over directly. Many doesn't mean all, however, which is why you should run the Windows 10 Upgrade Advisor prior to initiating the upgrade. The Upgrade Advisor will scan your current system and let you know what will be making the transition and what won't. Things that will not transfer over include some types of virus software, child safety settings and desktop gadgets. Windows Media center will also be

5

removed and a replacement call Windows DVD player will take its place. Games including Hearts, Solitaire and Minesweeper will all be removed with new versions available in the Windows Store. MDM functionality is not available in Windows 10.

Back up personal files with a recovery drive
When preparing to upgrade to Windows 10 it is important that you create a manual backup of your system, just in case something goes wrong. Running the Windows Recovery Tool prior to starting the new operating system installation is a good idea. This tool will create a backup of your currently installed operating system at its factory settings, be sure to back up personal files separately.

Get started
After you have done what you can to ensure your update goes as smoothly as possible, click on the Windows 10 icon in your taskbar and chose to start the upgrade. This will reserve your copy of Windows 10 from Microsoft while at the same time starting the download. If the download doesn't begin automatically, instead go to the Windows Update menu where the Windows 10 upgrade button should be waiting for you. If you do not wish to keep any of your existing data, you may also start a clean install of Windows 10.

If the option to upgrade is not appearing, try the following steps
- Search for Windows Update by using the search feature on the start menu.
- Select the option for how updates are installed before choose the important updates option.
- Choose the option to install recommended updates in the same way as important updates.
- Choose the Microsoft update option before choosing give me updates for other Microsoft products when I update Windows.
- Open the command prompt as an administrator and type wuaucit.exe/updatenow.
- The update should begin downloading.

Clean Install

- The first thing you must do is write down your Windows 10 product key and find a flash drive with at least 4 gigabytes of space available. Your product key can be found in the confirmation email you should have received from Microsoft when you elected to upgrade.
- Head to Microsoft.com and do a search for the ISO for Windows 10. This link will let you find the installation data copying tools you are looking for.
- Head to Rufus.akeo.ie and download the required software you need to put the data from Microsoft.com onto your flash drive.
- Put the flash drive into your computer and run the Rufus.akeo.ie program to create a Boot Disk.
- After the file has transferred, restart your computer before selecting the boot options menu (generally by pressing F2 or F12) when given the chance. Choose the flash drive when given the chance and you should see the installation menu for Windows 10.
- Choose your preferred language and choose custom install to perform a clean install.
- Choose the unallocated space option to delete your current partitions and let the installation begin.
- Insert your product key when asked.

Dual boot

If you are interested in running Windows 10 in addition to your current OS, the following steps are required:

- Make sure you have at least 20 gigabytes free on your hard drive.
- Make a new partition on your hard drive by using the command prompt and typing diskmgmt.msc.
- Choose a portion of free space by right clicking and choosing the New Simple Volume Option. When setting the size of the new partition make sure you set it in megabytes not gigabytes.
- Follow the onscreen prompts and select format partition when prompted to finish creating the partition
- Head to Rufus.akeo.ie and download the required software you need to put the data from Microsoft.com onto your flash drive.

- Put the flash drive into your computer and run the Rufus.akeo.ie program to create a Boot Disk.
- After the file has transferred, restart your computer before selecting the boot options menu (generally by pressing F2 or F12) when given the chance. Choose the flash drive when given the chance and you should see the installation menu for Windows 10.
- Choose the custom installation option and pick the new partition as the installation destination.
- When you boot the computer you should then be able to choose which operating system you boot into.

Delete the Old OS

After you have decided that Windows 10 is for you and that there is no going back, deleting the previous operating system can save space. When doing this be sure to copy over any relevant files, as they will not be salvageable after.

1. Use the search function in your start menu and search for Disk Cleanup Utility.
2. Chose the option to clean up system files near the lower left side of the screen

Find the old OS, typically housed in the C drive before looking for the folder holding prior installations of the Windows OS. Deleting this file will recover up to 20 gigabytes of space.

2 Windows 10 Interface

The Windows 10 interface offers up a wide variety of improvements when compared to prior versions across a myriad of common interface functions.

Improved Start Menu
The first thing you will likely notice when you boot up Windows 10 for the first time, is the radically different start menu. Windows 8 replaced the traditional start menu with a series of tiles, which received new information in real time. Public disapproval of the change brought the traditional start menu back, but Windows 10 brings back its most useful features.

The new start menu offers up many of the old standards including commonly used applications (the new word for programs) and power options, settings and file explorer. Up to 10 applications can be pinned to the start menu for quick access. The search function is also still intact though it now searches the Internet using Bing in addition to your personal files. More information on the other new search features can be found in chapter 3.

Instead of expanding out into a complete list of programs, the start menu now expands to show a wide variety of the live tiles that premiered in Windows 8. These tiles provide a wide variety of information that is updated in real time and includes things like social media alerts, weather forecasts and commonly viewed websites. Live tiles can be customized by determining how many tiles are shown and how big they are. They can also be turned off completely.

Microsoft Edge
When it comes to the user interface, there are no bigger changes that come along with Windows 10 than the way users are able to access the internet by default. The new browser is known as Microsoft Edge and it aims to fix all of the problems that people have been having with Internet Explorer for nearly a decade. The new browser takes inspiration from modern, lightweight browsers like Opera or Google Chrome. By default, Microsoft Edge is pinned to the new start menu and it pulls in any existing Internet Explorer data. Edge is designed for use across all of the Windows 10 platforms which means it has a simple to intuit interface with prominent, forward, back and reload buttons and few extras to get in the way.

Settings have also been paired down to the necessities, which includes determining how articles look while you are reading them, the list of websites that appear when you open the browser and options for new tabs. Themes and favorites options are also available. Private browsing is also an option, which allows you to browse websites without any of their information or data usage being recorded.

Opening the browser from the start menu is also possible by simply typing in a desired search and letting Windows 10 do the rest. The window that opens won't have the traditional navigation bar at the top though it will appear when you click in the area it typically occupies.

Reading Mode: Another new browser option is known as reading mode. While reading any article, a quick press of the reading mode button at the top of the screen will pull the article into a new window devoid of distractions like adds. Reading mode can be modified in the settings menu.

Top 10 Things in the new Windows 10

Sanyam Jain
The [TECH] Reverie

Top 10 Things in the new Windows 10

Windows 10
Following are the Top 10 new features of Windows 10 that will make you fall in love with it.
without any delay let's begin

Reading List: Despite the similar name, the reading list and reading mode aren't related. Instead, the reading list is similar to your list of Favorites, and lets you have a place to put interesting articles you want to read in their own area so as to not clog up your standard favorites with one-off links. Choosing the reading list icon from the navigation bar will present all of your reading list items as thumbnails for easier selection. Like favorites, reading list selections can be configured to show up when the new tab option is selected.

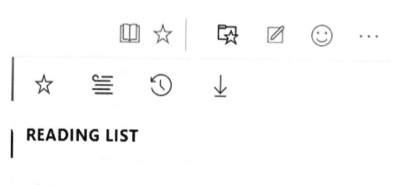

READING LIST

Today

Enhanced download protection: The downloads page in Microsoft Edge looks the same as those of its primary competitors in that it lists the files you are currently downloading in an interactive list. Microsoft Edge takes download security a step farther by automatically running a virus scan on programs that are being downloaded to ensure they are not going to harm your system.

Additional search functionality: At any point while viewing the Internet using Microsoft Edge, you can select a portion of text and use the enhanced search functionality to find out more information on your selection. This will then open a new window with more information on the topic from Wikipedia or similar sources. It will also list Windows 10 Apps that might be useful in conjunction with the website you are currently viewing. It can also find directions, menus and coupons depending on the context of the site you are viewing.

Annotations: While using Microsoft Edge to view websites you also have additional options when it comes to taking notes. You can now make notes on the webpage itself before posting the results online for everyone to see. This is done by clicking the pen-marking-up-paper icon from the navigation bar which will make the upper part of the browser change color while placing more options including a highlighter, a notation tool that looks like a pen, an eraser, a tool for writing more structured notes in boxes and one used for cropping. a mouse or a touch input will control all of these tools. Once you have finished making notations you can then save your work and share it online as it is automatically stored in the crowd. Sharing the results using Microsoft OneNote will also provide you with the option to allow other people to edit what you have done adding another level of interactivity to group projects undertaken online.

TRICKS   FACEBOOK   BLOGGER   GAME TWEAKS   DESIGN   GOOGLE

u Are Here : Home » Tricks, Windows » How to Disable Automatic Updates in Windows 10

How to Disable Automatic Updates in Windows 10

Posted by: Ashish Kumar   Posted date: Wednesday, 2 September 2015   In: Tricks, Windows

Unlike the previous versions of Windows operating system, you can't disable updates in

3 New Features of Windows 10-Cortana

Meet Cortana

Cortana first appeared on Windows phones and has since expanded to become a primary part of the Windows 10 experience. To ask Cortana a question, click on the search option found near the bottom left of your screen and type or speak a question (if you have a microphone). Cortana is available as soon as you start up Windows 10 with no additional effort required.

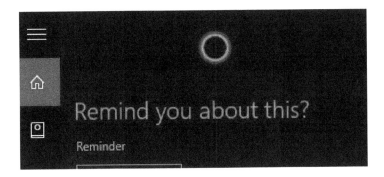

You will find that the Cortana system understands numerous commands for simple questions such as finding out about the day's forecast to taking notes, finding directions, taking reminders, pulling details on songs and determining the outcome of dice rolls or coin flips. It will also keep track of things like music and television preferences in order to alert you to local events you might like in your area. As long as you have a microphone, Cortana can be accessed by simply saying "Hey Cortana."

Having Cortana store personal information is optional, though it is turned on by default. Personal data stored includes contact information, interests and common locations; all of this information can be deleted from what is known as Cortana's notebook. To disable data collection search for Cortana's notebook and deselect the number one option.

Windows Store

Another holdover from Windows 8, the windows store is now the primary way you interact with and personalize your Windows 10 experience. Applications downloaded from the service are available across any compatible platforms and feature traditional program options like minimization and maximization. The Windows store also offers up options to replace many of the programs and gadgets that did not make the cut when switching over to Windows 10. Games downloaded from the Windows store are also available for play on the Xbox One.

Virtual Desktop

Users running multiple monitors will notice a number of features, which are designed to make their lives easier. First and foremost, the taskbar now allows user to filter out the applications that are not running in that particular window. To take this idea a step further, simply left click on the button next to the search option, which is known as the Task View button. When pressed, this button will bring up the current list of virtual desktops and windows that are currently in use.

If you are creating a virtual desktop for the first time, clicking this button will bring up the option to add a new desktop. Each new desktop can have its own list of programs running in order to keep order amongst disparate tasks. This feature has replaced the traditional Tab key + Windows key functionality from previous versions of Windows with a much more elaborate system. Pressing these keys, a single time, will allow you to see your current desktop as a thumbnail while pressing it again will switch to the next desktop which will have its own set of windows. These windows can also be navigated using the arrow keys. When looking at a list of desktops, the one with the line underneath it is the one, which is currently selected.

Windows can be moved between active desktops by opening the task view mode and right clicking on the program you wish to move before selecting the move option. Desktops can also be closed in this same way. Active windows in a closed desktop will be moved to an active desktop. This option is also available on Windows 10 tablets and mobile phones by swiping left from the main screen.

Enhanced Window Snapping
Windows 7 introduced the ability to snap a pair of windows to the desktop simultaneously. Windows 10 improves on this feature by letting you snap windows into the 4 quadrants of the screen while also allowing windows that are snapped to change size in relation to the size of the other snapped windows. A new snap assist feature will also provide you with a list of additional windows that can be snapped, even across desktops, when you snap the first window.

You can also now initiate a pair of snapped windows by pressing the Windows key + either the left or right arrow depending on the side of where you want the window to snap. What's more vertical snapping is finally an option and it can be initiated by either dragging a window up or down on the monitor or by pressing the Window key + the down arrow or the up arrow. Pressing either set of Windows + arrow key commands a second time will maximize the window in the direction pressed and doing it a third time will minimize it. Using the Windows key and the arrow right or left, then Windows key and the arrow down or up will put the selection into the corresponding quadrant.

Tablet Mode

Windows 10 is striving to unify the disparate products that currently run Windows and the inclusion of what is known, as Tablet Mode is central to this idea. You can activate it by selecting settings, in order to change the normal Start menu into a full screen option much closer to that of the traditional Windows 8 interface. This is the same mode that turns on automatically a phone and a tablet that are not connected to a keyboard. In this mode the Start Menu takes up all of the screen and works as the primary interface for the device. This holds true for the, the Applications Menu, the Settings Menu and the Windows Store. The desktop proper is not available in this mode but its contents can be found in the folder labeled desktop.

4 How to Make Windows 10 More Productive for You

Customize the start menu

- The star menu can be resided by placing your mouse on the upper right edge of the menu and pulling it where you want it to be.

- Live tiles can be unpinned from their position and new ones can be moved to replace them by right clicking on them. This also provides you with the option of changing their size or turning them off or on entirely.

- To place a new application on the start menu, select the all apps button before choosing the application you wish to pin and right clicking on it to place it on the start menu.

- Applications can also be pinned to the start menu's left side. To do this create a shortcut of the application before dragging it to where you want it to be. You will know it is in the right place once it displays itself as part of the start menu. These items can also be reordered by dragging them into the order you prefer.

- Right clicking on any application that is on either the left or right side of the start menu will let you remove them from their current position. Items, which are on the left side of the menu, can be dragged to the right side but items on the right have to be turned into shortcuts before they can be dragged left.

- You can add more buttons to the start menu by selecting properties from the menu that appears when you right-click on the desktop. Next choose the start menu tab before selecting the customize option. Extra buttons that can be added include documents, control panel, downloads and more.

- The Windows 8 mode can be found under personalization.

- These options apply to mobile Windows 10 as well, simply hold and press instead of right clicking.

Lock screen functionality

Windows 10 also provides new options when it comes to personalizing the lock screen. This can be done with either a specific picture or a slideshow, similar to the traditional background. The slideshow also has a variety of options to ensure that the pictures that are shown always look their best. The lock screen now also has the ability to shown up to 7 different application live tiles to allow you to view up to date information without unlocking your computer.

Create Keyboard shortcuts

Creating your own keyboard shortcut for commonly used applications will save you time every time you open them. This can be done by first creating a shortcut for the application. The easiest way to do this is to drag the application to the desktop from the start menu. After creating the shortcut, select it by right clicking on it to reveal its properties. Chose the option for creating a shortcut before typing the desired shortcut. Shortcuts must start with CTRL and Alt and then include a letter, number or function key.

Create an application

Creating a Windows 10 application is quite simple as long as you have a specific use in mind for the application you are creating.

- Start by choosing the settings menu from the start screen before choosing the security and updates option followed by the developer mode option.
- With this done, head to http://appstudio.windows.com/en-us and use your Windows Live ID to log in.
- Choose the Windows 10 option to be presented with relevant templates for your applications.
- Name your application and then decide what type of information your application will pull from the Internet. This includes social media feeds, HTML code or RSS feeds.

- From there you will be given options to change how the content looks in the template you choose and allowed to change other aspects of the application as well.
- Next you will be given the opportunity to set the live tile options for the application so it can be pinned to the start menu or the lock screen.
- Clicking finish will let the website create the application before giving you a link to download it for your very own. You will also be given the option to download the source code for the application if you are interested in creating something that is a little more complicated.
- Download the file to your desktop before unzipping the file and opening it.
- Right click on the option marked Add-AppDevPackage and selecting the option titled Powershell.
- Follow the resulting instructions and your application should be ready to use in a matter of minutes.

Deeper Personalization Options
Additional personalization options can be found by exploring the settings menu. This will provide you with the ability to alter a number of preset options, many of these options are cosmetic, including the ability to set up your own slideshow as your screensaver or as your background image.

You will also be presented with the option to change the color of your start menu as well as the border around windows. There are a wide variety of preset colors as well as the option to let Windows 10 decide on the appropriate color based on what would positively accent your selected background image. These options can also be made to include the start meu color, the action center color and the taskbar color. This will also provide you with the option to make these three solid or transparent.

Found under the heading titled related settings, the options for Windows themes remain largely unchanged since Windows 7. New features include increased options when it comes to colors and sounds. This is also the place that things like icons, mouse pointers, screen savers and sounds are now changed. Selecting the theme menu and tweaking the existing settings as you see fit can also create personalized themes. Themes can also be saved locally or exported and shared with friends.

5 Accounts and Security

Windows 10 offers up a host of new account and security features designed to ensure your Windows 10 experience is as personalized and secure as possible.

Microsoft ID
The first additional security feature comes in the form of a Microsoft ID account, which will allow you to access information stored in the cloud on any Windows 10 device while at the same time serving as the initial gatekeeper to your Windows 10 data. While already having a Microsoft ID is not listed as an official upgrade requirement, not entering one when prompted has been known to cause installation issues. To set up a Microsoft ID, go to the settings menu, click on change PC settings, accounts and finally, my accounts. This menu will provide you with the opportunity to connect an existing Microsoft ID to the current system or to create one from scratch.

Windows Hello
If your system uses either a biometric scanner or RealSense 3D technology, you can set these security features to allow you to completely bypass the traditional login screen. Known jointly as Windows Hello, these features are activated by going to the settings menu, followed by accounts and finally, sign-in options.

Set your privacy settings
By default, Windows collects a wide variety of user data, ostensibly to monitor and improve the Windows 10 experience. To prevent it from doing so, you must alter your privacy settings. Reach the privacy settings menu by going to the settings menu and selecting the privacy option. On the privacy menu you can determine how your Windows 10 device tracks your microphone, camera, location data and more. It is also important to choose the diagnostic/feedback button and selected a feedback frequency of

never and usage and diagnostic data level. These two options will ensure the data Microsoft collects from your account will be both negligible and minimal.

Protect your browser history
By default, Microsoft Edge sends your Internet history to Microsoft with the goal of helping Cortana make your user experience unique and personally tailored to you. If this sound a little too much like Big Brother for your tastes, consider going into the Microsoft Edge settings menu before choosing Advanced Settings, view advanced settings and finally, services and privacy before selecting the option which turns off the option to allow Cortana to assist you off. Turning off the page prediction feature, which claims to make your experience better, improve reading and speed up browsing as it also collects most of your data.

Avoid making a Microsoft Account
Despite the similarity in name and function, a Microsoft Account is not the same as a Windows ID. If you are interested in preventing Microsoft from tracking all of your data, skipping the Microsoft Account creation step is recommended. Opting out of a Microsoft Account will allow you to keep more of your information on the device you originally added it to and prevent Microsoft from creating a central hub to connect all of your metadata too.

If you do create a Microsoft Account, make sure you thoroughly read the privacy policy first. If you already created a Microsoft Account, it can be deleted from the settings menu, simply choose the accounts option and then the option marked your account to access the ability to delete your account.

Don't let Cortana snoop
While the Cortana search function can prove useful in a wide variety of situations or when it comes to personalizing your Windows 10 experience, it does collect a fair amount of data. Cortana is programed to learn about all of your wants and needs, which means it is constantly monitoring everything you do on your

Windows 10 device. This includes handwriting patterns, speech patterns, commonly used contacts and location data as well as Internet usage. What's more, this information is stored in the cloud, not necessarily the safest place for it to be.

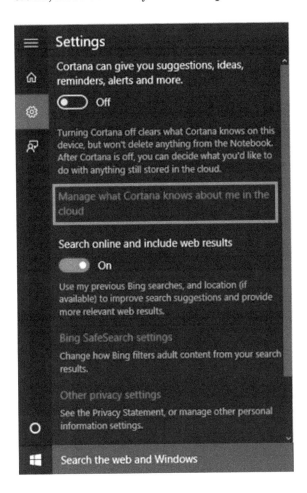

In order to opt out of all of Cortana's help, simply pull up the search function options and clear the list of typing, thinking, talking, typing and interest data entries.

6 Advanced Tricks

If you find that third party products, such as printers, aren't working after the upgrade...
The simplest fix for this sort of issue is the same fix that has worked for over 20 years, all you need to do is uninstall the drivers for the device in question, and reinstall them. The new drivers don't even need to be Windows 10 specific, as reinstalling just forces Windows 10 to recognize the device. To do this you simply choose the devices option in the control panel, find the device in question and click on the option to remove it. Once it has been removed, simply go online and find the drivers for the product in question and reinstall.

If you find that you are suddenly low on virtual memory after the upgrade...
This is most likely due to the fact that Windows 10 allocates less RAM to virtual memory than most previous versions of Windows did and it can create performance issues.

To fix this issue, start by entering the control panel before finding the option relating to performance. The next step is to choose the option which includes modifying appearance and performance, before selecting advanced options. Finally, select the virtual memory option and ensure the box next to the option to automatically mange the size of paging files is not checked. With this done it is up to you to choose the drive where you installed Windows 10 and select the option to change the paging size. At this point Windows should offer up some size maximums that is best if you accept. A restart will be required to make this process take affect.

If you want to skip the login screen...
By default, Windows 10 makes you sign in every single time you want to access your device. To stop it from doing this open the

command line by pressing the R KEY and the WINDOWS KEY. Type in netpllwiz and press the ENTER KEY. From there it is simply selected the appropriate user and ensure the enter username option is not selected. From there, type your password in the box titled automatically log on. Ensure you apply the changes and you are good to go.

If you find that many of your files are now defaulting to new programs...
This is most likely because all of the file types reverted to their original programs along with the update and you changed the defaults at some point so long ago that you no longer remember. The program you were using may also not yet have a Windows 10 version, which is the solution you should try first.

If that isn't the case, then at least changing the file back to your preferred settings is much easier than with previous versions of Windows. All you need to do is right click on a file whose defaults you want to change and choose the option labeled open with. From there select "choose alternative application" option and determine how you want that type of file to open in the future. Select the option to always use the selected application option if you don't want to have to go through this process every time you open that file type.

If your bookmarks didn't auto-populate into Microsoft Edge...
Without a doubt, Microsoft put more effort into the redesign of its native web browser than just about any other facet of the new operating system. That doesn't mean it is perfect however and if you suddenly can't find your old bookmarks, or if you just want to include bookmarks from a second browser as well, the solution is relatively simple. First head to the options menu, which now looks like three separate lines and locate the option to import favorites. From there all you have to do is to choose which browser you wish to import the bookmarks from.

To make Windows 10 boot from a cold state more quickly

After you have upgraded to Windows 10, if you find that it suddenly seems to take much longer for your device to cold boot than it used to, there are a number of possible reasons to consider.

Applications are sucking up resources
One of the most likely culprits for this type of problem, especially if it seems that the boot times keep getting longer, is that applications you are starting are automatically configured to start whenever the operating system boots up. As such, each new application you run means your computer will take longer and longer to start each time it is restarted.

To stop this boot creep in its tracks, find the task manager and open it before choosing the option to see additional details. From there, navigate to the tab labeled startup, which can be found at the top of the screen. Look for the status column to find a list of all of the applications, which have to start before your system finishes starting. Select the disable options to pare down this list until you have only the essentials starting when the computer does and you should see results as soon as you restart the computer for your choices to take effect.

Services are sucking up resources
If you find that cutting back on your running applications doesn't make your system boot all that much faster, consider looking into which services are constantly running in the background, constantly putting a drain on all of your system's resources. To determine which services are currently running, press the WINDOWS KEY and the X KEY to open the window dedicated to managing services. Choose the computer management option then applications and services. This can also be found by choosing the option labeled my computer before choosing manager, or simply right clicking on the PC icon on the Windows 10 desktop.

Once you have accessed the services manager you will find a list of all of the currently running services active on your devices. When switching services from automatic, it is important to switch them to manual and never to off. As long as they are set to manual then Windows 10 can turn them on when it needs to access them.

Services, which can be safely set to manual without hurting system integrity include:

- *Connected User Telemetry and Experiences:* This is one of only three systems that can be completely turned off without incident as all it does is allow Microsoft to collect and monitor your data for their own purposes.
- *DMWApPushSVC:* Turn this off as it relates to how Microsoft collects and monitors your data for their own purposes.
- *Tracking Service Diagnostic:* The final system you can completely turn off, it relates to how Microsoft collects and monitors your data for their own purposes.
- *Diagnostic Service Policy:* Rarely used, set it to manual.
- *Windows Search:* Can be safely turned to manual or off if you never use it.
- *WIA (Windows Image Acquisition):* can be turned to manual and is only used if your device takes pictures.
- *Error Reporting Service for Windows 10:* This is in charge of sending crash reports and other errors to Microsoft.
- *Windows Defender:* Even if you have other virus software, this should still be set to manual as it can cause errors otherwise.
- *Handwriting service panel and touch keyboard:* Depending on what type of device you are using to run Windows 10.
- *IP NetBIOS/ TCP Helper*: As long as you are not connected to network based workgroup.
- *Security Services*: Depending on your need for system security.
- *Remote Registry:* If you are worried about your system being remotely hacked then set this to manual or even disabled.
- *Printer Spooling:* this can be set to manual but shouldn't be disabled if you want the device to be able to connect remotely to printers in the future.
- *Assistant Service for program compatibility:* Should be set to manual as it allows certain applications to interface properly.

- *IP Helper:* Required if you use an IPv6 connection, can be set to manual otherwise.
- *Maps Download Manager:* Useful if you use the integrated maps application. You should disable it if you don't want Windows 10 to know your location.
- *Distributed Client Link Tracking:* This can be set to manual if your device does not connect to a network.

Too much stress on your video card

- If your slowdown does not appear to be services or application related, the next place to look is at the current level of animations and visual flourishes Windows 10 provides. Tweaking these visual enhancements can result in noticeable improvements when it comes to completing common tasks. To change which visual options you can see, start by pressing the R KEY and the WINDOWS KEY to bring up the command line prompt. Type sysdm.cpl into the box before hitting enter. Open the advanced options menu and select performance, followed by settings. This menu will allow you to alter a wide variety of visual properties including:
The frequency and depth of drop shadows
- How boxes look as they scroll
- How combo boxes are interacted with
- If selections are reflected visually
- If shadows can be seen on windows
- If the mouse pointer has a shadow
- How thumbnail previews are saved and displayed
- If menu items fade when clicked upon to indicate they have been clicked
- Decide how and when tool tips appear
- Decide how and when menus appear
- Set the level of animation that is displayed in the taskbar
- Decide how it looks when windows are either minimized or maximized
- Set the rate of animation and interactivity that affects open windows

After your selections have been made, select the option to apply them before closing the window. If you are interested in switching all of the Windows 10 specific animation options off at once, you can simply press the I Key and the WINDOWS KEY before selecting the option marked ease of action under the other tab. From there you simply select the play animations option and turn it to the off position.

There is also an option to determine the level of transparency that the start menu exhibits along with the taskbar and action center. Start by selecting the personalization option from the start menu before selecting colors, then choosing the option to set the level of transparency.

Fancy Folders
The final reason you may be experiencing unexpected slowdown is that you have to many features running in the folders you are opening. To change these features, start by opening the application label This PC which can be found, among other places, on the desktop. Select the option labeled folder before selecting tab labeled view. Deselecting the options that are selected will help your folders respond more quickly to your commands. Don't forget to click apply before closing the window.

Bring back classic programs
While the Windows 10 applications have their uses, some people will also long for their favorite program that did not make the transition to the current platform. While tracking down the program of your dreams does take some effort, it can be done with a bit of perseverance and by following the steps suggested below. The first step to bringing back your favorites is to delete the new applications.

This is harder than it sounds however as none of the native Windows 10 applications can be removed by default. To get around this fact, simply download the program called CCleaner by going online to PiriForm.com/CCleaner/download. This program is great for removing temporary files that may be clogging up your system and the latest version allows users to removed unwanted applications as well. After you have downloaded the program and let it run for the first time, open up the tools tab to find the option for deleting applications.

If you are interested in removing all of the applications installed on the system at once, you don't have worry about downloading Ccleaner. That is because this process is available through a program known as PowerShell which is already installed on your system. To access this program simply use the search function to find it. Before clicking on the program make sure to open it in Administrator mode by pressing the CTRL KEY, the SHIFT KEY and the ENTER KEY. This can also be accomplished by choosing the option to run the program as an administrator from the right click menu.

This screen might look a bit intimidating at first, but the options you have are rather limited. To uninstall all of the applications that are currently installed across all users, type in Get-AppxPackage before typing Remove-AppxPackage. This option is not recommended however as unilaterally removing applications is known to cause a variety of stability and functionality issues that are hard to predict. Uninstalling individual applications using the PowerShell is also an option. This is ideal if you do not have access to CCleaner. The appropriate commands for each application can be found below:

- *Skype Video and Windows Messaging applications uninstall* (Type get-AppxPackage* messaging* and then type remove-AppxPackage)

- *Sway application uninstall* (Type Get-AppxPackage*sway* and then type remove-AppxPackage)

- *Phone application uninstall* (Type get-AppxPackage*commsphone* and then type remove-AppxPackage)

- *Phone Companion application uninstall* (Type get-AppxPackage*windowsphone* and then type remove-AppxPackage)

- *Phone and Phone Companion application uninstall* (Type get-AppxPackage*phone* and then type remove-AppxPackage)

- *Mail and Calendar application uninstall* (Type get-AppxPackage*communicationsapps* and then type remove-AppxPackage

- *People application uninstall* (Type get-AppxPackage*people* and then type remove-AppxPackage

- *Groove Music application uninstall* (Type get-AppxPackage*zunemusic* and then type remove-AppxPackage

- *Television and movie application uninstall* (Type get-AppxPackage*zunevideo* and then type move-AppxPackage

- *Television, Movies, Groove Music application (Entertainment Collectively)* (Type get-AppxPackage*zune* and then type remove-AppxPackage

- *Money application uninstall* (Type get-AppxPackage*bingfinance* and then type remove-AppxPackage

- *News application uninstall* (Type get-AppxPackage*bingnews* and then type remove-AppxPackage

- *Sports application uninstall* (Type get-AppxPackage*bingsports* and then type remove-AppxPackage

- *Weather application uninstall* (Type get-AppxPackage*bingweather* and then type remove-AppxPackage

- *Money, News Weather and Sports application uninstall* (Type get-AppxPackage*bing* and then type Remove-AppxPackage

- *OneNote application uninstall* (Type get-AppxPackage*onenote* and then type remove-AppxPackage

- *Alarms & Clock application uninstall* (Type get-AppxPackage*alarms* and then type remove-AppxPackage

- *Calculator application uninstall* (Type get-AppxPackage*calculator* and then type remove-AppxPackage

- *Camera application uninstall* (Type get-Get-AppxPackage*camera* and then type remove-AppxPackage

- *Photos application uninstall* (Type get-AppxPackage*photos* and then type remove-AppxPackage

- *Maps application uninstall* (Type get-AppxPackage*maps* and then type remove-AppxPackage

- *Voice Recorder application uninstall* (Type get-AppxPackage*soundrecorder* and then type Remove-AppxPackage

- *Xbox application uninstall* (Type get-AppxPackage*xbox* and then type remove-AppxPackage

- *Microsoft Solitaire Collection application uninstall* (Type get-AppxPackage*solitaire* and then type remove-AppxPackage

- *Office application uninstall* (Type get-AppxPackage*officehub and then type remove-AppxPackage

- *Skype application uninstall* (Type get-AppxPackage*skypeapp* and then type remove-AppxPackage

- *Get Started application uninstall* (Type get-AppxPackage*getstarted* and then type remove-AppxPackage

- *3D Builder application uninstall* (Type get-AppxPackage*3dbuilder* and then type remove-AppxPackage

- *Windows Store application uninstall* (Type get-AppxPackage*windowsstore* and then type remove-AppxPackage (not recommended)

After you have removed the programs you have no use for, you can then proceed to track down older options using the techniques described below. If the program you are longing for is not listed below, there is still hope. Trying searching online and odds are someone has preserved it somewhere. Good luck!

- *Calculator:* The advanced calculator from Windows XP still works with Windows 10. To find it, simply head to Microsoft.com and search for the Calculator Plus file. Choose the classic mode and you are good to go.
- *WordPad:* This only works if you still have the older version of Windows on your Windows 10 device. Open the command line as previously discussed and type in C:\Windows\System 32 followed by the ENTER key. Search for the file named wordpad.exe.
- *MS Paint:* This only works if you still have the older version of Windows on your Windows 10 device. Open the command line as previously discussed and type in C:\Windows\System 32 followed by the ENTER key. Search for the file named mspaint.exe.
- *Internet Explorer:* Internet Explorer is a legacy program which means it is included in Windows 10 to ensure some older programs function properly. If you wish to continue using it, simply look for it in the application titled Internet Explorer.
- *Windows Photo Viewer:* If you upgraded from an earlier version of windows than Windows Photo Viewer is still accessible. To access it, right-click on a photo, choose the default application option and choose Windows Photo Viewer as the default option.

•

7 The Fun Part of Windows 10-Apps-Xbox Application

Streaming considerations

Those who have access to both an Xbox One as well as a Windows 10 capable machine have the ability to stream their Xbox One and some Xbox 360 games onto their computer; providing both devices are connected to the same wireless network. There is some lag between the systems though it is not enough to make single-player games unplayable. Games played in this fashion will be able to benefit from the enhanced graphical fidelity available on personal computers, assuming the wireless network they are connected to is up to the task. Wireless Xbox One gamepad support is also available exclusively on machines running Windows 10.

DVR
Games aren't the only thing that can be streamed from the Xbox One, as coming in 2016 it also picks up standard HDTV channels like ABC, NBC and CBS for no additional fee. These broadcasts can then be streamed to any other Windows 10 device. The Xbox One also functions as a DVR and recorded shows can also be streamed to anything else of the same wireless network. Recordings can also

be downloaded to any Windows 10 device.

Other entertainment options

Windows Groove
Windows Groove is the preinstalled music application that allows you take control of your music and playlists across all of your interconnected Windows 10 devices. Groove can be downloaded and accessed from any PC, Windows 10 phone, iPhone, Xbox or any Android device. It also offers ad-free access to over 40 million songs for a monthly fee.

Movies and TV application
The Movies and TV application lets you rent or purchase a wide variety of HD content directly from Microsoft. The benefit of this is that anything your rent or purchase is available across all of your Windows 10 devices, with viewing details synched so you can seamlessly switch from one to another.

8 Keyboard Shortcuts

Press the WINDOWS KEY to bring up the Start Menu for Windows 10

Press the Tab Key and the WINDOWS KEY to bring up the Windows 10 task view

Press the Q Key and the WINDOWS KEY to bring up the speak with Cortana

Press the S Key and the WINDOWS KEY to search with keyboard input

Press the I KEY and the WINDOWS KEY to bring up the Windows 10 settings

Press the A KEY and the WINDOWS KEY to bring up notifications

Press the K KEY and the WINDOWS KEY to lock your Windows 10 device

Press the D KEY, CTRL KEY and WINDOWS KEY to create a virtual desktop

Press the F4 KEY, CTRL KEY and WINDOWS KEY to close virtual desktops

Press an ARROW KEY, CTRL KEY and WINDOWS KEY to switch desktops

Press an ARROW KEY and the WINDOWS KEY to position snapped windows

Press the H KEY and the WINDOWS KEY to share selected content

Press the K KEY and the WINDOWS KEY to connect to wireless devices

Press the X KEY and the WINDOWS KEY to open the start button context menu

Press the G KEY and the WINDOWS KEY to open the Windows 10 Game Bar

Press the D Key and the WINDOWS KEY to show the current desktop

Press the E Key and the WINDOWS KEY to activate Windows Explorer

Press the SPACE BAR Key and the WINDOWS KEY to switch preset languages

Press an ARROW KEY plus SHIFT and the WINDOWS KEY to switch monitors

Press a NUMBER Key and the WINDOWS KEY to open pinned programs

Press the R Key and the WINDOWS KEY to run a command

Press the P Key and the WINDOWS KEY to project a screen

Press the ALT KEY AND THE TAB KEY to switch to a previous window

Press the ALT KEY and the SPACE BAR to manipulate the current application

Press the ALT KEY and the F4 KEY to close an app or shut down the system

9 Conclusion

Thank you again for ordering this book! I hope this book was able to help you to get a better grasp on the intricacies of Windows 10. While it may look different on the outside, inside it is largely the same operating system that it has been for more than two decades. With that being said, it will still most likely take you several hours before everything begins to feel normal.

The next step is to persevere through this awkward phase, stop reading and start taking advantage of all the new features that Windows 10 has to offer. Take the plunge and get ready to upgrade your system, your phone, tablet or PC will thank you.

Finally, if you enjoyed this book, then I'd like to ask you for a favor, would you be kind enough to leave a review for this book on Amazon? It'd be greatly appreciated!

Thank you

.

ABOUT THE AUTHOR

Jonathan Bates is the founder of Tech talk books and has been a computer enthusiast for over 20 years. After graduating from the University of East Anglia, Norwich and gaining his masters degree at Imperial College, London in Computer Engineering, Jonathan worked at major technology companies across Asia and the U.S.A. In 2014 he decided to settle back to his native home, London. He now works as a computer programmer and has developed a love for writing articles and books, having discovered that many people don't understand the fundamentals of getting the most out of their software. His passion for programming comes out in his writing, which he is currently in the process of writing a series of programming books

www.ingramcontent.com/pod-product-compliance
Lightning Source LLC
Chambersburg PA
CBHW060933050326
40689CB00013B/3067